SCOTLAND

LAND OF BEAUTY

SCOTLAND
LAND OF BEAUTY

DONALD SOMMERVILLE

MAGNA
BOOKS

Published by Magna Books
Magna Road
Wigston
Leicester LE18 4ZH

Produced by Bison Books Ltd.
Kimbolton House
117A Fulham Road
London SW3 6RL

ISBN 1-85422-798-X

Printed in China

The right of Donald Sommerville to be identified as the
author has been asserted by the same in accordance
with the Copyright, Designs and Patents Act 1988.

Page 1: The bonnie banks of Loch Lomond, celebrated in one
of Scotland's best known songs.

Pages 2-3: The ruined ramparts of Castle Urquhart overlook
a ship on Loch Ness. The loch is the longest and one of the
deepest in Britain and its dark waters, complicated currents,
and temperature variations make it less than transparent to
even the most modern observation techniques. What better
place for a monster to hide in?

Below: Although Linlithgow Palace has long been a ruin, its
former grandeur is still readily to be appreciated from this
view across its handsome park. It was begun under James I,
around 1425, but was remodeled and extended at various
times up to the reign of James VI & I around 1620. By the end
of the seventeenth century, however, it had begun to fall into
disrepair.

Below right: The lower slopes of Scotland's highest
mountain, Ben Nevis, viewed from just outside Fort William.

Overleaf, page 6: The Grey Mare's Tail Waterfall among the
richly wooded hills near Newton Stewart is one of the best-
known beauty spots in the south west.

Overleaf, page 7: A black-faced sheep looks down on one of
the lighthouses dotting the rugged coast of the Mull of
Kintyre.

CONTENTS

INTRODUCTION

IN RECENT MONTHS A traveler crossing the frontier from England into Scotland by the main west coast route, the A74 road, would have been entirely unable to tell where the border was because there was no obvious change to mark the transition – even the 'Welcome to Scotland' signs were missing (albeit temporarily, because of road works). Yet the traveler would soon be in little doubt that this was a nation with a dramatic individual history, a vigorous and unique culture, and a varied landscape of unsurpassed beauty and grandeur.

The same visitor might be surprised to see that very few Scotsmen wear the kilt on a regular basis and that not every town has a castle on one side of its principal shopping street, as Edinburgh has, while the shops on that street would not seem greatly out of place in London, England, or even London, Ontario. Many Scots, indeed, are cynical about the tartan and whisky image that so readily attaches itself to their country and its culture, but many of the same Scotsmen are proud to be married in a kilt (usually hired for the event) – which, when you think about it, is an interesting nationalist statement to make about oneself on an important personal occasion.

I, who write these words, am a Scot. I was born and brought up in Glasgow, but I have worked in London (the English one) for roughly half my life and, as the saying goes, some of my best friends are English. When traveling abroad I have often been asked by new acquaintants, "Where are you from?" I invariably reply "I *live* in London," since this is the information that is being sought, but if we talk longer I

will make it clear that "I am *from* Scotland." Equally when I visit my family or friends in Scotland I think of it as going home. And I am sure, beyond doubt or argument, that once in Scotland, the air is purer, the grass greener, the scenery nobler and the people uniquely distinguished by their generosity, humor, sobriety and other fine qualities.

The attachment of the expatriate Scot to his or her country is, of course, one of the clichés of Scottishness. "Yet still the blood is strong .... And we in dreams behold the Hebrides", is how one famous poem of emigration, *The Canadian Boat Song*, has it, and throughout Canada, and any other place where there are people of Scots descent, there are St Andrew's Societies and Burns Suppers. Scots are quick to boast of their country's qualities and will even claim that this sentimental attachment is proof of some special virtue, for who has ever heard of an expatriate Englishman (and we love to tease the English) celebrating Shakespeare's birthday?

Leaving aside the sentimentality, in fact we do not need to boast. Independent judges have nominated places in Scotland as World Heritage Sites, while others are renowned for their natural beauty and importance to conservation. In my heart I may believe that Scotland cannot be bettered, but in my head I know that, whatever I may feel, we do have much that is very good and very fine indeed. This book is intended to be a celebration of precisely that, to be enjoyed by Scots, expatriates, and foreigners alike and to show any doubters just what we Scots get so excited about.

LANDSCAPES

SCOTLAND'S LANDSCAPE is one of the country's most prized assets. "I look upon Switzerland as an inferior sort of Scotland", is the description of one famous writer, reflecting the place of the mountain scenery of the Highlands as the finest and most famous in the country. The characteristic picture of Scottish scenery is of an open, heather-clad hillside, home to grouse and red deer or perhaps a few sheep, but this is far from a universal scene, the softer rolling outlines of the Border hills providing one contrast and the gentler farmlands of the Lowlands a still greater change.

Indeed, many of the lower slopes at least of the northern hills were once covered with the mixed woodlands of the old Caledonian forest of which only the smallest remnants now remain. In recent years many hillsides have again become tree-clad but, this time, unfortunately, from the scenic and conservation point of view, with the dreary, identical ranks and alien species of commercial forestry.

Scotland's highest mountain, Ben Nevis, stands 1344 meters high by the latest measurement (but many Scots still remember its traditional and now evidently inaccurate height of 4406 feet) – a modest peak indeed when compared to the summits attained by the continental ranges of Europe, North America and elsewhere. This reflects the age of much of the land.

The rocks of the north and west are some of the oldest on the planet and, if the geologists' ideas of continental movements are correct, were once in the southern hemisphere. Much more recently in geological terms most of Scotland was ground under the glaciers of the Ice Ages as can be seen in many of the landforms.

The Victorians, led by their Queen, were notable for their enjoyment of Scotland's scenic beauties and present day Scots are enthusiastic in this cause also. Scotland is fortunate that there is a long tradition of free public access to wild or uncultivated land, so Scots and visitors alike can readily enjoy the rich variety of scenery and experience that is available. Ben Nevis can be climbed by the not-too-demanding tourist path to magnificent views on a fine summer's day while its north-facing buttresses and gullies offer rock and ice climbing of the highest standard for those who are suitably prepared.

The gentler loch and upland landscapes of the Trossachs of Stirlingshire and Perthshire or the Pentland Hills of the Lothians offer still more accessible delights. Or what indeed could be more definitively Scottish than an evening view across the golf links at a modest east coast town or the quiet bustle at a west coast harbor with fishing boats unloading and the island ferry about to sail?

Overleaf, page 8: The Old Man of Stoer is a famous coastal landmark on the wild coast of the north west, north of Lochinver. Its spectacular column of rock towers some 200 feet above the waves that lap its base.

Overleaf, page 9: The shaggy and pugnacious-looking Highland cattle are no longer prominent in the agricultural economy but are still widely kept.

Right: Cannon on the bastions of Edinburgh Castle dominate the town. It is from here that the traditional One O'Clock Gun is still fired to remind citizens who may have forgotten their watches what the time is. The weapon used nowadays is not one of the veteran pieces nearer the camera, but the modern design seen at the farthest angle of the battlements.

Left: The well-kept harbor of Pittenweem, one of a group of charming fishing villages along the south coast.

Below left: The bleak and open landscape of a crofting community on Canna, in the Inner Hebrides.

Right: One of the ubiquitous Caledonian MacBrayne ferries makes the short Mull-Iona crossing. In fine weather the water here has a remarkable, clarity, reinforcing the atmosphere of calm and sanctity for the visitor approaching Iona, heart of one of the earliest Christian communities in Scotland.

Below right: Brightly painted buildings along the sea front at Tobermory, the largest town on Mull.

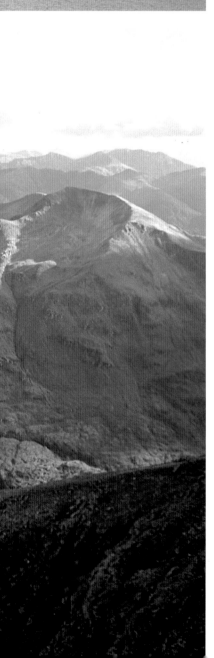

Top left: Loch Shiel lies beautifully calm, bathed in late summer sunlight, in a photograph taken from beside the Jacobite monument at Glenfinnan at the head of the loch.

Left: The view east from the top of Ben Nevis. Many of Scotland's finest hillwalking, scrambling and climbing routes can be found in the rugged expanse of wild and roadless country that lies to the east of Scotland's highest peak.

Above: Wild flowers bloom among the bogs and lochans of Rannoch Moor. Some 60 square miles in area, and roughly 1000 feet above sea level, Rannoch Moor is a seemingly vast expanse of beauty and desolation.

Left: The golden eagle is the grandest and most elusive of Scotland's birds. This young bird seems to sense the carefully concealed presence of the photographer. Many visitors to Scotland hope to spot a Golden Eagle but most have to content themselves with the smaller and much more common buzzard.

Below left: The red grouse is a noted game bird. This example can be readily seen among the conifer foliage, but among the moorland grasses of its more usual habitat its camouflage is very effective indeed.

Below: The capercaillie is also of the grouse family but can be clearly distinguished by its black plumage.

Right: A group of red deer high on the Cairngorm plateau above Aviemore.

Top left: The small village of Shieldaig lies on Loch Shieldaig, an arm of Loch Torridon in Wester Ross. Many good judges would describe the mountain scenery of Torridon as the finest in the land.

Left: The high Cairngorms are one of Scotland's great mountain wildernesses, a harsh and demanding landscape indeed in such wintry weather as this, but providing, too, only a short distance away, Scotland's most popular ski slopes.

Above: Although less elevated than the famed Cuillin range farther south on the island, the Quirang on the Trotternish peninsula in the north of Skye also provides a range of dramatic landscapes for the visitor to admire.

Left: Purple heather clothes the hillsides near Braemar. By late summer or early fall, when this picture was taken, the hillsides of the Highlands take on a subtle and handsome blend of browns and purples to delight the eye of any onlooker.

Below: Early morning light and mist on the hills, a quiet lochan and an old stone bridge on the road – a picture of peace in a small Sutherland community.

Right: The River Morar makes its short and rapid plunge from Loch Morar to the sea. The loch is the deepest in Britain, over 1000 feet at one point, and it, too, is said to conceal a monster.

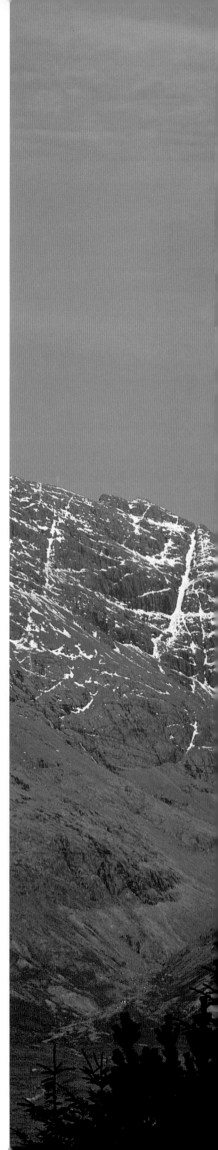

Top: Restored traditional thatched houses at a folk museum on the Isle of Skye. The thick rough stone walls and thatch well weighted down were and still are essential to give protection against Atlantic gales.

Above: Loch Pityoulish in Inverness-shire in the almost eerie glow of an early morning mist.

Right: The Black Cuillins of Skye. From this picture it is easy to see why the Cuillin range is renowned for providing some of the finest rock climbing in Britain. Less adventurous visitors can still admire its dramatic and forbidding scenery.

Left: The glorious white sands of Balnakeil Bay on the far northern coast near Cape Wrath.

Below: Razorbills and a lone scavenging gull crowd the ledges of a west coast cliff. The cliffs and islands of Scotland provide a precarious but evidently highly suitable refuge for vast populations of sea birds.

Left: Pleasure craft on the Caledonian Canal at the south end of Loch Ness at Fort Augustus. Designed by the great engineer Thomas Telford, the Caledonian Canal links the lochs of the Great Glen and provides a passage from the Atlantic to the North Sea avoiding the stormy northern route.

Right: Lighthouse on Fair Isle. Fair Isle lies between the Orkneys and the Shetlands and is nowadays most visited by ornithologists to view its huge population of sea birds.

Below: The cliffs of Cape Wrath, north-westerly tip of the Scottish mainland.

Above left: A cottage on the Orkneys. This old Norse earldom lies off the north coast of Scotland and comprises over 70 islands.

Left: The last house at Scotland's north east extremity at John O'Groats attracts a regular stream of visitors throughout the year. The unusual name comes from a Dutchman, John de Groot, who made his home here in the time of James IV.

Above: The church on Fair Isle standing strong and square against the winds of the Atlantic and North Sea. Fair Isle is owned by the National Trust for Scotland, and although it is less than four miles long, over 300 species of birds have been sighted there.

HISTORY

LIKE MANY OTHER small countries bordered by a larger, richer and more powerful neighbor, Scotland's history has been overshadowed by that relationship, in this case with England. However, with brief exceptions, Scotland successfully retained its independence from the formation of the country to the union of the Scottish and English crowns in 1603 and in some respects beyond then to 1707 and the union of the Scots and English parliaments. In the nearly three centuries since, Scotland has maintained its own legal, educational and religious systems. Through these, and the continuing vigor of its native traditions, it has continued to have a distinct history and identity and may yet return to a more independent political position.

Scotland has a rich legacy of archeological remains, most commonly found in the northerly Orkney and Shetland Islands, from the earliest periods of human history, but naturally it is the sites and artefacts of more recent centuries which survive in greatest profusion and which attract greatest interest.

Three great themes have underlain the drama, tragedy, and romance of these more recent centuries and have interacted to provoke the many bloody quarrels with which Scots history is littered. First, of course, has been the fluctuating struggle with England for independence which has often been linked with the second concern, the attempts of Scotland's rulers to assert their authority over powerful lords throughout the country and the usually lawless and violent Highland clans in particular. Finally there has been religion and the creation of the various Protestant churches, their internal organization, and the place of the Protestant and other traditions in public life.

The universal human problem of making a living in a harsh landscape and a changing economy has underlined these themes. For Scotland this has meant the development and subsequent decline of various traditional lifestyles. During the nineteenth century, much of the population of the Highlands was notoriously and brutally cleared on to the emigrant ships for Canada or to the Victorian slums of Glasgow to make room for the Cheviot sheep or the red deer which would maximize the former clan chiefs' income. A similar process of change has happened in the towns. Glasgow has built successive periods of economic growth first on the tobacco trade, then the cotton industry, and later, in its industrial heyday, making ships and locomotives. All of these have now largely passed away leaving an uncertain future.

What is certain is that Scotland's colorful past gives much to enjoy and relive whether it is the proud defiance of Bannockburn or the noble tones of the Declaration of Arbroath at the height of the Wars of Independence, the disappointed hopes of Bonnie Prince Charlie and his Jacobite clansmen or the poignancy of evicted Sutherland clansfolk scratching parting messages, still legible 150 years later, on the windows of the church where they had taken refuge before beginning their disconsolate journeys to the south or Canada or Australia. Above all, the role of Scotland and the Scots in the affairs of the world has been out of all proportion to the size and population of the country and that, at least, is something to be proud of.

Above left: Iona Abbey. Iona was the site of the monastery founded by St Columba around AD 563. Columba, however, was not the first to bring Christianity to Scotland, for St Ninian had come to Galloway more than one hundred years before. Iona still somehow retains an air of calm spirituality and is nowadays the home of an active and far-flung Christian community.

Left: Melrose Abbey suffered much in the English wars before finally being destroyed in 1544. Established by David I in the twelfth century, it was a Cistercian foundation.

Above: Edinburgh Castle takes on a less martial aspect when seen from the gardens below that separate it from the town's principal shopping street, Princes Street.

Right: Jedburgh Abbey, like Melrose, was destroyed in 1544 in the 'Rough Wooing' when Henry VIII sent armies to force the Scots to allow a marriage between his young son Edward and the infant Mary, Queen of Scots.

Overleaf, page 30: The ruins of St Andrews Cathedral. Built between the twelfth and fourteenth centuries, the cathedral was burnt in 1599 by the Protestant army of the Lords of the Congregation in their struggle with Mary of Guise, mother and regent for Mary, Queen of Scots.

Overleaf, page 31: The magnificent eighth century cross at Kildalton on Islay.

Left: Kilchurn Castle by Loch Awe, established in 1440, was for long a stronghold of the Campbells of Breadalbane. The same gale that swept away the original Tay Bridge in 1879 also demolished a tower at Kilchurn.

Above: Greenknowe Tower, built in 1581, a typical fortified house of the Borders.

Left: The Palace of Holyroodhouse in Edinburgh is the Queen's official residence in Scotland. Most of the present palace was commissioned by Charles II in 1671 from the architect Sir William Bruce. The palace is built in a neo-classical style but the front, shown in the photograph, combines this with elements of the traditional tower house.

Below left: The ruined castle of St Andrews, once the palace of the Archbishop. It was held for over a year in 1546-47 by Protestant reformers who included John Knox. They eventually surrendered to besiegers including a French fleet and Knox was taken to France to serve for a time as a galley slave.

Right: This house on the High Street in the Old Town of Edinburgh is known as John Knox House. It is not certain if it has a direct connection with the religious leader although he is believed to have lived on the second floor from 1561 until dying in the house in 1572. The house itself dates from around 1490.

Below: Linlithgow Palace is now ruined but was described by Mary of Guise, wife of James V, as the finest palace she had seen. Perhaps her attitude was influenced by other factors. Mary and James celebrated their wedding at Linlithgow and the fountain in the Quadrangle is said to have run with wine for the occasion. Their only child Mary, Queen of Scots, was born here in 1542.

Left: Eilean Donan Castle on the shores of Loch Duich was the ancient seat of the Macrae clan. During the brief Jacobite rebellion of 1719 it was bombarded by Hanoverian forces. The Jacobites had assistance from a small Spanish force but most of the clans did not join the rising and it was easily defeated at Glen Shiel nearby.

Below: The old bridge over the River Coe at Glencoe. In February 1692 after the chief of the MacDonald clan of the glen had failed to take an oath of loyalty to King William he and many of his people were killed by government soldiers from the Campbell clan, the MacDonalds' traditional enemies. The Campbells first accepted hospitality from the MacDonalds before turning on them suddenly by night. The incident achieved notoriety as the Massacre of Glencoe.

Left: The fifteenth century Castle Campbell in Dollar Glen was once the principal seat of the Campbell clan.

Right: A disused church on the small island of Canna in the Inner Hebrides. Depopulation has left even the famously devout highland and island communities unable to support the churches they once sustained. Even small communities may have several churches, usually a reminder of the disruptions and splits which fragmented the Presbyterian faith in the nineteenth and early twentieth centuries.

Below: A traditional croft building at a museum on Skye. The oldest type of thatched house would not have had any windows as this example has or even a proper chimney.

Above: The village at New Lanark was established by the industrialist David Dale who built a mill, powered by the water of the Clyde, and housing for his workers there. Dale was reckoned a philanthropic employer and his successor as proprietor, Robert Owen, took this strand still further during his ownership from 1800-25.

Left: The Glenfinnan monument was built in 1815 in memory of the highlanders who died during the 1745 Jacobite rebellion. Bonnie Prince Charlie, raised his standard at Glenfinnan as the rebellion began.

Right: The Glenfinnan Viaduct on the Fort William – Mallaig rail line was built in 1898.

Left: Balmoral Castle on Royal Deeside. Queen Victoria had a lifelong passion for the Scottish Highlands, delighting in the peace and solitude of the scenery and the romance of its historical associations. She and Prince Albert had the castle at Balmoral built in 1853-56 and it still remains the favorite summer holiday destination of most of the royal family.

Below: Scotland's martial history did not end with the country's absorption into the United Kingdom. In World War II parts of the Highlands were extensively used as training grounds for special forces' units. The picture shows the Commando Memorial commemorating this at Spean Bridge north of Fort William.

Right: The Forth Bridge is a grand statement of the skill of the Victorian engineers who built it in 1883-90. The little island seen under the middle of the bridge is Inchgarvie which was fortified in 1779 to defend against a threatened attack by John Paul Jones, founder of the US Navy, who was, of course, a Scot.

BUILDINGS

FINE AND HANDSOME buildings and a distinctive architectural tradition and native styles are among Scotland's best, but perhaps least-known attractions. Two architectural names stand out from the crowd and deserve their international fame – the Adam family and Charles Rennie Mackintosh. It is perhaps also typical that Robert Adam, the most brilliant of the clan, specifically stated that he found Scotland too narrow a stage on which to work and consequently created relatively few of his finest designs at home, while Mackintosh's talents were long little appreciated in the country of his birth.

Robert Adam and his talented brothers gained some of their early experience assisting their father, William, in the government contracting aspects of his business. A number of the bridges, roads and forts constructed to pacify the Jacobite Highlands bear the family's mark, a token of the fact that many of Scotland's most notable structures fall into fields that are perhaps better described as civil and military engineering rather than architecture. The basic principles on which most roads are constructed even today were, indeed, set out by a Scot, John Loudon Macadam, and bridges and canals built by his contemporary Thomas Telford can still impress. Later feats of civil engineering like the Forth rail and road bridges are also among Scotland's most distinctive landmarks.

One group of buildings, combining civil and military functions, can be said to be uniquely Scottish in style, the tower houses built by noble and gentry families to combine the functions of residence and defensive stronghold. Scotland has comparatively few great castles and few indeed that survive in any notable state of preservation. Many were destroyed in the English wars and others were dismantled by kings like Robert the Bruce who recognized that they were most likely to be effective as centers for alien rule rather than serve as bulwarks of defense. More modest tower houses, by contrast, are far more common and some of their rich variety can be seen in the following pages.

Churches and other religious buildings are another repository of the architectural heritage, but here too much has been lost to the ravages of time and foreign and home-grown vandalism. Most famous are the border abbeys, largely destroyed during Henry VIII's 'Rough Wooing' of 1544-45. The remaining noble fragments in their beautiful settings still give tantalizing glimpses of what once was. Other cathedrals and monasteries were at best neglected, and at worst quarried for their building stone in the aftermath of the Reformation and the Protestant reformers' disdain for the symbols of Roman pomp and authority.

Humbler buildings will be more familiar to many Scots, whether the sandstone tenement flats of Glasgow, Aberdeen's traditional granite or the thatched houses of the western highlands. Glasgow's tenements were for long the targets of the planners' demolition men but thankfully, are now being restored and refurbished. It is easy to be cynical about the work of town planners, but Glasgow's rival Edinburgh can claim to have been favored by at least one town planning success, the glorious Georgian New Town which fully merits its worldwide reputation.

Overleaf, page 48: Castle Sween in Argyll is believed to be the oldest stone castle on the Scottish mainland, dating in part from the late eleventh century.

Overleaf, page 49: The sign outside the modern-day Deacon Brodie's Tavern in Edinburgh. Brodie lived a double life: by day a wealthy and respectable pillar of society, by night a gambler and adulterer, who paid for his vices by a life of crime.

Below: Kelso Abbey, founded by David I in 1128. Architecturally it stands at the transition from the Romanesque to the Gothic style, but the older Romanesque predominates.

Right: St John's Cross and Iona Abbey. There are numerous remains of early Christian times on the island of Iona but the abbey itself is largely the product of modern restoration work.

Left: Crathes Castle, just inland from Aberdeen, was begun in 1553 and largely completed in 1594. Its various wings and more generous allocation of windows reflect a greater attention by this time to domestic comfort and less to defense. As well as its fine exterior architecture, Crathes also boasts an interesting interior including a range of superb painted ceilings.

Below left: Dryburgh Abbey, another casualty of Henry VIII's 'Rough Wooing'. As well as its architectural interest, Dryburgh Abbey is also the burial place of the writer Sir Walter Scott.

Below: Braemar Castle was built an an old site by the Earl of Mar in 1628. It was garrisoned by Hanoverian troops after the 1715 and 1745 Jacobite rebellions. The musket loopholes they made in the curtain wall can still be seen.

Above left: Floors Castle is the home of the Dukes of Roxburghe. It was designed and built by William Adam in 1721-25 and extensively remodeled by William Playfair in the 1840s. It is the largest, and probably the grandest great house in Scotland.

Left: Glamis Castle. An original, plain fourteenth century tower house is at the heart of Glamis Castle which was granted to its present owners, the Lyon family, in 1372. The best known modern member of the family is Queen Elizabeth, the Queen Mother who, as Lady Elizabeth Bowes-Lyon, had her childhood home here.

Above & right: Two views of Culzean Castle in Ayrshire, one of the finest of Robert Adam's designs in his native Scotland.

Right: Mellerstain House, near Kelso in the Borders. Mellerstain shows the handiwork of two members of the Adam family. The wings of the present house were built first, from 1725, to a design by William Adam, and the central block in the 1770s to a scheme by his son, Robert. Robert Adam's beautiful designs for the interior of the main public rooms have been carefully maintained.

Above: The characteristic working class, and often middle class dwelling in Glasgow was the tenement flat.

Left: Glasgow University moved in 1870 from its ancient site in the center of town to a magnificent location on Gilmorehill in the west, overlooking Kelvingrove Park. The main building, shown here, was designed by George Gilbert Scott.

Right: Victorian office buildings in Hope Street in the center of Glasgow's business district, built in the city's characteristic red sandstone to a bluff, confident, no-nonsense design that reflected the city's current economic growth and success.

59

Above: Kinloch Castle on the tiny island of Rhum is one of the grandest of the sporting retreats built in the Highlands and islands in the Victorian and Edwardian eras. The island of Rhum was inherited by Sir George Bullough, of a family of Lancashire industrialists, in 1891 and he commissioned his new castle from the London architects Leeming and Leeming. The building itself is in a lavish fantasy Baronial style. It is said that Sir George completed the picture by paying his workmen (who were mainly English craftsmen shipped in especially) a supplement to their wages for wearing the kilt while they worked. Certainly no expense was spared; the house cost around £250,000 at the time, a huge sum when converted into modern values.

Left: The coat of arms of the city of Glasgow. The tree, the fish, the bell and the ring in the design all relate to miraculous events in the life of St Mungo, the city's patron saint, who is believed to have established a church at 'Glasgu' (the beloved green place) around 550AD.

Above right: Decorative banners in George Square in the center of Glasgow. The city's grand municipal building, the City Chambers, completed in 1888, is situated in George Square.

Right: The decorative ironwork on this Glasgow lamppost also features parts of the city emblem.

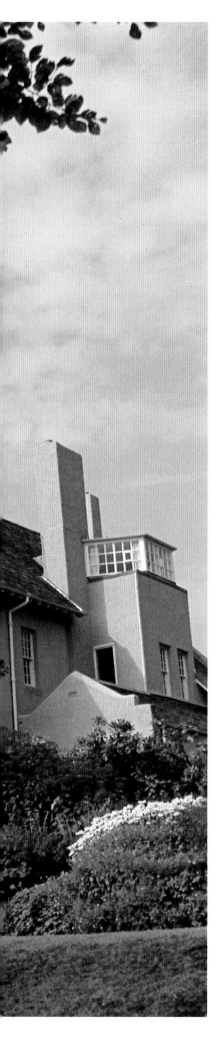

Left: The Hill House in Helensburgh, designed throughout by Charles Rennie Mackintosh in 1902. The building's exterior style reflects a number of elements in the traditional architecture of the Scottish tower house, particularly the turret and conical roof,

and the geometric relationship of the various wings of the house.

Below: If the exterior of The Hill House has traditional features, the interior, designed to the last detail by Mackintosh, was undoubtedly innovative.

This is the White Bedroom; carpet, furniture and fittings all contributing to an elegant, harmonious whole.

Bottom: Still serving their original function are the Willow Tearooms in Glasgow's Sauchiehall Street, another Mackintosh design.

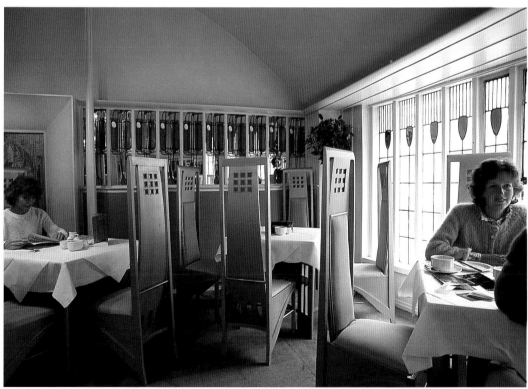

Left: The Scotland Street School in Glasgow. The boundary walls and decorative iron fencing round the site are partially obscured by the modern street furniture in this photograph, but the lines of the main building can be seen to good effect with, once again, the circular towers and conical roofs of Scottish tradition, combined with the strong verticals characteristic of much of Mackintosh's work. The building is now used as an educational museum and is much visited by the city's school children and others to experience life in the classroom in Edwardian times.

PEOPLE & TRADITIONS

SCOTLAND, THE HOME OF GOLF and Scotch whisky, of haggis and tweed, highland games and the Edinburgh Festival. These are a few of the best known facets of Scottish life and, if they are not all workaday concerns for every Scot, their place in the tourist guides is justifiable since most Scots will admit to enjoying some of them without too much outside encouragement. Like traditions everywhere, some can claim a genuine and ancient history, others would do better to keep quiet. No one knows who first distilled whisky or when (and since it may well have been the Irish it can be passed quickly over) and a game known as "goff" was popular enough in the fifteenth century to be banned by law because it interfered with archery practice essential to the nation's defense. Kilts and tartan are much newer, largely deriving their modern forms from some very dubious nineteenth century historical "research". The Edinburgh Festival may only have a few decades of tradition as yet, but it makes up for this defect by its overall quality and the ability, year in, year out, of some of the more radical performers on the Fringe to outrage the city's staider citizens and more pompous officials and thereby amuse everyone else.

As well as such internationally-known events there are smaller affairs that reflect the variety of the Scots heritage and, less influenced by the marketing men, are maybe more genuine and more fun. Ceremonies like the Common Ridings held in a number of Border towns reflect a more martial past, while Up Helly Ah in the Shetlands is a reminder of the significant Norse influence in these northerly isles.

A major part of the Scottish heritage business is naturally concerned with the truly astonishing number of Scots who have achieved great influence in every field of human endeavor. Scots will tell you that they invented everything worth inventing, from the steam engine to television, or the waterproof raincoat to penicillin. Amazingly, it is a boast that is nearly true. The American economist J.K. Galbraith once commented that the only race to have achieved anything like as disproportionately large a role in the world's affairs as the Scots were the Jews. Modern governments would do well to remember the reason why – that from the sixteenth through the nineteenth century Scotland's public education system was the best in the world, and widely available to all classes in society.

But that is too sensible a note on which to leave an introduction to the traditions of the nation that gave caber tossing to the world. The Scots have as great a capacity as anyone to enjoy the quieter and the more ridiculous pleasures in life. Join us in these and we will soon know and like each other better.

Overleaf, page 66: The still house in the Fettercairn malt whisky distillery. Fettercairn is in the Howe of the Mearns in the former Kincardineshire. The distillery produces a Highland malt. In malt whisky distilling many factors contribute to the flavor of the eventual product. Crucial is the actual shape of the still which will affect the taste even when the water and

other parts of the process remain constant.

Overleaf, page 67: Willie Auchterlonie won the British Open Championship in 1893 and his family clubmaking business in St Andrews still exists. The early professionals often combined the trades of greenkeeper and clubmaker with their playing.

Left: The malting house at Glen Garioch distillery, Old Meldrum, Aberdeenshire.

Below left: The Edradour distillery at Pitlochry is Scotland's smallest and was established in 1837.

Below: The opening moments of a shinty match. Shinty is a fast and furious field hockey type game

played in the highlands and islands. It has been suggested that exiled Scots in Canada adapted their native game to be played on ice and thereby created ice hockey. A shinty match begins, as here, when the referee throws the ball high between two opposing players and, if he has any sense, jumps away before they attempt their first strikes.

Left: A judge and a competitor confer among the cabers at Blairgowrie Highland Games.

Right: Throwing the hammer at Nethybridge Highland Games. The so-called 'heavy events' are the best known of the attractions at highland games but there are invariably also competitions for highland dancing, pipe bands and individual pipers.

Below: Caber tossing, seen here at Paisley Highland Games, is uniquely Scottish. The aim is to have the caber flip end over end in an exactly straight line and one of the entertainments of the event is to watch a competitor staggering through his run-up, while the judge anxiously bobs around to try to stay in line and assess the throw correctly.

Below: Not all of Scotland's courses are in the grand championship style. This is a scene at Brodick golf club on the island of Arran, a favorite holiday destination in the Firth of Clyde. The course here is short, mainly being composed of tricky par-3 holes, but is handsomely positioned by the beach and overlooked by the island's principal hill, Goat Fell.

Right: The home of golf, the Royal and Ancient Golf Club of St Andrews, viewed from across the 18th green of the famous Old Course. The Old Course, and others in the town, are in fact municipal courses and welcome visitors from all around the world. The fact that 18 has become the standard number of holes on a golf course is owed to the original layout of the St Andrews course.

Top: Salmon fishing on the Tay near Dunkeld. Many of Scotland's major rivers are famed for the quality of their fishing, which unfortunately is reflected in the expense of a day's fishing on many of the best beats.

Above: A different sort of wildlife displays its distinctive markings at an Edinburgh Festival event. The Edinburgh Festival combines top-flight musical and theatrical performances by international stars with the varied delights of the Fringe.

Right: Fireworks burst over the center of Edinburgh. The Castle stands in the background. Another popular feature of the Festival events is the Military Tattoo of pipe bands and other displays produced on the Castle Esplanade.

Above: Tartan skirts on sale, carefully labelled with the appropriate clan label. Tartan sellers will solemnly research the 'correct' pattern for visitors with the least Scottish of names if they so desire.

Left: Pipe band members in Edinburgh's Princes Street. One of the traditions of the Edinburgh Tattoo is of the lone piper on the battlements of the castle who plays at the closing moments of the display.

Right: A fishing boat unloading at Scrabster, on the north coast near Thurso. Herring fishing was one of the traditional backbones of the Scottish economy in former times.

77

Right: Cranes on the River Clyde at Glasgow silhouetted by the setting sun. The River Clyde was once the world's premier shipbuilding center with yard after yard along the banks at Glasgow and further down river, while the port carried the city's heavy engineering products and the men who made them all around the world.

ACKNOWLEDGMENTS

Editor: Judith Millidge
Picture Researcher: Suzanne O'Farrell
Design: Design 23

The author and publisher would like to thank the
following individuals and institutions for permission to
use the photographs on the pages noted below.

AA PHOTO LIBRARY, pages: 4, 7,30, 32 (bottom),
33 (both), 36 (top), 37 (below), 42 (top),
50, 52, (below), 54 (top), 56-57, 61 (below), 64-65, 66,
67, 68 (top), 73.

ANCIENT MONUMENTS OF SCOTLAND, page: 31.

GLASGOW DISTRICT COUNCIL, page: 58.

LIFE FILE, photo © David Baliss: page 6;
© Graham Burns: pages 12 (below), 13 (both), 16
(bottom right), 18 (top), 20 (below), 27 (top), 29, 35, 37
(top), 40, 41 (top), 48, 49, 59 (both), 60 (both), 70
(below), 74 (below), 75, 76, 77 (top), 78-79;
© Elizabeth Crowe: page 36 (below);
© Joe Evans: pages 1, 44;
© Caroline Field: pages 20 (top), 52 (top), 53, 54
(below), 70 (top), 74 (top);
© Ron Gregory: pages 19, 34, 68 (below);
© Bob Hughes: pages 2-3, 26;
© Mo Khan: page 72;
© Malcolm Parker: page 55 (below);
© Ian Richards: page 27 (below);
© Paul Richards: pages 8, 10-11, 22 (top), 23, 24, 41
(below):
© Richard Robinson: pages 12 (top), 47;
© W. Shakell: page 9;
© Fergus Smith: pages 16 (top and bottom left), 17, 18
(below), 21, 25, 30 (below), 46, 69, 71;
© Cliff Threadgold: pages 5, 14 (top), 42 (below) 43;
© Jean Unsworth: page 39;
© Andrew Ward: pages 14 (below), 15, 28 (top), 38,
77 (below).

NATIONAL TRUST OF SCOTLAND, pages 32 (top),
51, 55 (top), 62-63.